BREAKING THE CORPS LINE

THE STORY OF BLACK BALLERINA LLANCHIE STEVENSON

MINA AHMAD-CROSBY

LANDA & WILDAN PUBLISHING

Copyright © 2021 by Mina Ahmad-Crosby

All rights reserved.

No part of this book may be reproduced in any form or by any electronic or mechanical means, including information storage and retrieval systems, without written permission from the author, except for the use of brief quotations in a book review.

Cover design by Abdul-Malik Ahmad.

Photo Credit: Marbeth

CONTENTS

Foreword ix
Introduction xi

1. Arriving to America 1
2. Learning to Dance 9
3. Dancing Professionally 17
4. Classical Training 25
5. Creating a Legacy 32
6. Guided by Faith 40
7. Life after Ballet 48

Timeline 54
Key Figures 56
Bibliography 59
Acknowledgments 77
About the Author 79

To Llanchie's grandchildren: Sakina, Salih, Siraj, Samina, Mezaan, and Raees. May you always remember her courage and continue to pray for her.

قال رسول الله - صلى الله عليه وسلم:
إن الله يحب إذا عمل أحدكم عملا أن يتقنه". حسن, رواه البيهقي

The Messenger of God
(peace and blessing be upon him) said:
"God loves that whenever any of you does something, they should excel in it."

(Hasan, Reported by al-Bayhaqi)

FOREWORD

My daughter Mina did not tell me she was writing a book. She simply began asking me questions about my life in text messages and our weekly Quran classes over Zoom. You can imagine my surprise when a draft of this book showed up on my doorstep! I had incredible parents who lovingly pushed me to excel, and I have beautiful children who have brought unmeasurable joy into my life.

I am delighted Mina decided to document my time as a ballerina. When asked about Llanchie Stevenson, I often think to myself, "I don't know - she is not me." My ballet career was only a short portion of my early years. My life as a Muslim mother spans almost half a century. However, in those few years, Llanchie left her mark on the ballet world forever.

I hope that readers, especially my grandchildren, are inspired by the story of a Black ballerina to pursue their passions, even in the face of significant obstacles. We are all given unique gifts and talents that can benefit our fellow human beings. Focus your intentions on helping others and work endlessly towards your goals!

Aminah L. Ahmad (formerly Llanchie Stevenson)

INTRODUCTION

Ballet as a form of dance began in Europe around the 14th century as a means for society's elite to celebrate momentous occasions. Over the next few centuries, the classic dance style was developed, moving from the ballroom to complex performances on stages by highly trained dancers. Ballet gained popularity in the United States after World War I with the influx of Russian immigrants around the 1930s. Schools and companies began forming initially in New York and California, eventually opening in most major cities across the country. For decades, segregation remained deeply entrenched in the American framework; African-Americans were routinely barred from accessing training and opportunities.

The number of successful Black ballet dancers such as Misty Copeland and Michaela DePrince is slowly increasing. Many men and women from previous generations helped set the stage upon which these dancers perform. One such courageous ballerina is Llanchie Stevenson. She dreamt of achieving fame and success as a principal ballerina in a major company. Although she encountered numerous obstacles due to her skin color, she worked tirelessly to break barriers where she could.

Her stage name, Llanchie, is used primarily throughout this book. Her name has changed numerous times throughout the years; a different moniker characterized each unique period in her life. In her journey, she danced for two of the most prolific American choreographers, Alvin Ailey under the name Rosemarie and Arthur Mitchell as Llanchie. When she retired to focus on her spirituality, she replaced her last name with the letter X. Entering into the folds of the second-largest religion in the world, she became known as Aminah Ahmad. Her story is one of a strong woman determined to pursue the life she envisioned for herself, both in the world of ballet and ultimately in her decision to live as a Muslim.

1
ARRIVING TO AMERICA

"The beautiful island of Trinidad is inhabited by peoples of many races, originating from many different lands. They have settled here for diverse reasons and, with the passing of time, have learned to live and work together." - Herbert Stevenson, father of Llanchie

LLANCHIE'S story begins near the Caribbean Sea and the islands touched by its warm waters. Her parents, Herbert and Ruby, resided in Port of Spain, the capital city of the British-controlled island of Trinidad. Known as *Lere*, the Land of the hummingbird, to its indigenous Arawak and Carib people, the tiny island is adorned with magnificent waterfalls and lush foliage. The gentle hum of the native bird was soon drowned out by noises of battle as forces of colonial Spain and Britain fought for control of the land, overpowering its native inhabitants. Destruction, then decimation ensued, with Britain rising triumphantly in 1797.

The climate and soil proved to be ideal conditions for growing sugar. Labor was imported, as the native populations were rendered extinct through war and infectious diseases introduced by the foreign invaders. To meet the demands of sugar plantations, Africans were enslaved and transported to the island until the 1830s, when Great Britain outlawed slavery. Herbert Barclay Stevenson and Ruby Griffith were two descendants of those enslaved Africans, muddled with British blood.

The young couple left their home of Trinidad in search of better employment opportunities, first to the island nation of Curaçao, then finally settling in the Dutch-controlled island of Aruba. A new oil refinery belonging to Lago Oil and Transport Company had recently opened in Aruba, capitalizing on the tremendous global demand for gasoline post-World War II. The company offered a myriad of jobs for the local Aruban population and inhabitants of its surrounding islands. Herbert began working in the refinery and living in the second largest city of San Nicholas. In contrast to Trinidad's lush greenery, Aruba's arid climate and modest rainfall produce a desert-like landscape. When asked what the island is like, Llanchie often described her birthplace simply as a "rock."

Family History

Llanchie's mother, Ruby, was the oldest of the four Griffith girls. She shouldered most of the responsibilities of raising her younger sisters when their mother died unexpectedly in childbirth. The family had to grieve not only for their matriarch but also for the twin boys she was carrying at the time. Ruby became the mother of the house at the young age of eleven. Having children of her own was never a strong desire, but she eventually married Herbert Stevenson and was soon pregnant with the child who would become their only offspring. After a hard and painful labor, Ruby finally delivered a beautiful baby girl on a warm Tuesday in February 1945.

Her parents named her Rosemarie Leanna Stevenson, commonly calling her by her middle name. In the years that followed, Leanna was shortened to "*Yana*." Her nickname was eventually lengthened by the addition of "*chie*", a word of endearment in the Papiamento language spoken in Aruba. When she would choose a stage name for a dancing career years later, Llanchie was born, using the Spanish letter "ll" to represent the "*y*" sound.

Although she was an only child, Llanchie grew up surrounded by her prominent, close-knit family members. Her parents shared a modest home with Ruby's sister Stella, her husband Peter, and their young children. Llanchie's cousin Candy was only nine months younger than her, and together they were raised like sisters. Ruby enjoyed social gatherings and would host parties and get-togethers often. The Griffith sisters were deeply committed to their Christian faith and instilled in their children the importance of service to God at a young age. Ruby's family, along with her sisters' families, were members of the Methodist church, and the Griffith sisters would organize most of the church's activities. They ran the Sunday School and coordinated the Easter and Christmas programs each year.

. . .

Llanchie enrolled in her first year of schooling in Aruba. She attended a Dutch school, where the teachers' prejudice was apparent even to a young girl. The teachers and administration seemed to favor her classmates had distinctly different features than her. One school day, a teacher reprimanded Llanchie for slight misbehavior and threatened to fail her. Llanchie smiled mischievously at the teacher and told her proudly, *"I won't be here next year! I'm going to America."* As punishment, Llanchie was forced to stand in the corner of the schoolhouse all day. Her classmates took pity on her and tried to whisper calming words in her direction, but the teacher quickly silenced their voices.

A New Country

Her father, Herbert, was a hardworking, proud man who was always striving to raise the economic standing of his small family. His first cousin, Ruby Abbensetts, lived in the United States with her small family, including a daughter also named Rosemarie. They had found relative success in carving out an upper-middle-class life in New York. Herbert, with help from his cousin, was able to immigrate to America. His employment search was successful, and he sent for his wife and daughter a short while later.

Upon arriving in New York City, the young Stevenson family spent one month living with Herbert's cousin in the middle-class neighborhood of Jamaica in the borough of Queens. Previously a predominantly Irish immigrant area, the 1950s saw an influx of middle-class Black Americans prompting the steady departure of the white families. Despite the everyday financial struggles of a newly immigrated family, Ruby and Herbert were determined to show their daughter the magic of their new home. Embracing the traditions of the land, they dressed her up for Halloween and brought a small $5 tree to put on a dresser for Christmas. Ignoring its tiny stature, they decorated and placed wrapped gifts around it. It snowed on her first Christmas Eve in the United States, the fresh blanket of snow amazed the young island girl.

The first years in the States consisted of living in shared apartments with other families. After staying with Herbert's cousin, the family moved into a one-room attic a few blocks down the street. They soon developed a close relationship with their neighbors, an elderly couple named Charles and Mildred Trotman. The two had wed later in life and had no children of their own. They enjoyed the laughter and light young children brought into their lives and became surrogate grandparents to all the neighborhood children. Once both parents were working, Llanchie was dropped off at a neighbor's house, where she would partake in a simple breakfast with the family. Mr. Trotman, affectionately called Grandpa by the children, would walk the kids to school and pick them up after the final bell of dismissal. Llanchie can recall many days when she would skip ahead of her Grandpa as they hurried to and from school each day. She would remain at the Trotman's house in the afternoons, where Mildred would give her piano lessons. After completing her homework, Llanchie would head over to her childhood friend Verna's home while Mildred cooked dinner, typically soul food with stuffing, greens, and cornbread.

Llanchie's parents were loving but very strict as they pushed her toward excellence. Her father would often tell her that she was better than both her White peers and American descendants of slavery because of her West Indies background. Her parents strongly emphasized education; her father led the example by attending night school after long days at the warehouse to obtain his bachelor's degree. slight concern was raised when she began second grade at the local public school near her home. Her teacher noticed that Llanchie would often reverse her letters when she wrote them. They assumed that this error was due to Llanchie's transition from the Dutch-only instruction she had received in Aruba. With encouragement from her kind teacher, Llanchie soon found her stride and performed well throughout elementary school.

As the years progressed, the one-room attic became too cramped. Herbert arranged to share a nearby townhome with a family called the Wilsons. Initially, when Llanchie and her parents moved in, the Wilson family was away traveling, leaving the entire four-bedroom house empty. Herbert warned Llanchie not to get used to these accommodations. Finally, when the Wilsons returned, Llanchie and her parents occupied two bedrooms, one converted into a living room and the other serving as their bedroom. Herbert used the small living room space as an office; Llanchie often found her father hunched over his desk late at night studying. He eventually achieved a high school diploma and completed an undergraduate college degree as well.

Llanchie intensely disliked living in this new home. Ruby had limited access to the kitchen, and the family would always complain that Llanchie was making too much noise. The Wilsons owned a television, and Llanchie would stand in the hallway watching from a distance. They knew she was there but never invited her into the room to join them. In fact, She felt they knew that her favorite show was Howdy Doody and would purposely turn the television off midway into the program. Childcare was another issue now that they no longer lived close by Grandpa Trotman. Ruby arranged for an older lady to watch Llanchie, but she mostly ignored the young child, often telling her to be quiet because she was reading her bible.

When Llanchie was 13, the family finally secured an apartment where Llanchie had her own bedroom. Her parents settled in East Elmhurst, Queens, where they rented for the remainder of their natural lives. With strong faith and determination, Llanchie's parents fell into a routine in the new country. While they came to the States without college degrees, their hard work and perseverance created a path for some career advancement. Herbert become a manager at a warehouse of household goods. Ruby was employed at a laundromat before having a long career, first as a clerk, then a medical secretary at Mount Sinai Hospital in Manhattan. While never reaching an abundance of monetary success, Llanchie took pride in how her parents spoiled and cherished her. She spent hours pouring over the most recent Sears catalog, cutting out pictures of all the toys, clothes, and other items she wanted. Her parents would utilize layaway; the items would eventually make their way to her.

Two of Ruby's sisters and their families immigrated to the United States, and Llanchie spent significant amounts of time surrounded by her many cousins. The family developed an extensive social network; her parents were active in a local Trinidadian cultural organization and were at church multiple times each week. Lance felt extremely loved by her friends and family. She reflects that even though money was always tight, her parents found the means to throw her a magnificent sweet sixteen party. Over a hundred friends and family from her school, dance studio, and church life attended the event.

2

LEARNING TO DANCE

"Education and work are the levers to uplift a people." – W. E. B. Du Bois

WHILE LLANCHIE GREW up with limited resources, her parents always made time for quality family moments. Despite their long hours at work or night school, they took her to the many sights and events occurring in New York City. When she was eight, her parents brought her to Radio City Music Hall to watch a performance. This venue was financed by philanthropist John D. Rockefeller, Jr. and hailed as the largest indoor theater globally at the time. Radio City Music Hall housed the Corps de Ballet, a ballet company that would perform alongside the famous Rockettes. The magnificent costumes and the graceful movements of the ballet dancers on stage enamored Llanchie. As she left the hall with classical music swirling around her head, she shared her desire to do ballet with her parents.

. . .

The Bernice Johnson Dance Studio

Llanchie's mother found the perfect place for her to begin taking ballet lessons. In the Southeastern side of Queens, a dynamic woman named Bernice Johnson owned a small dance studio. Bernice Johnson was an original chorus dancer in the Cotton Club, a premier nightclub that often featured the most popular black entertainers at the time. The club itself restricted its clientele; African-Americans were barred from enjoying the amenities during the first twelve years of its operations. She was a trendsetter in her own right as the first dark skin dancer at the Cotton Club; her talent and beauty were undeniable.

Mrs. Johnson began teaching in her basement and then grew her studio to a small, unassuming storefront. She was a savvy Black businesswoman who had a keen eye for developing young talent. Although she was not classically trained, her experiences enabled her to teach various classes, including tap, interpretive dance, and ballet. She taught the mechanics of specific movements and emphasized unique performance skills such as commanding a stage and captivating an audience. The success of her former students spans generations, including actor Ben Vereen, actress Valarie Pettiford, and singer/songwriter Ashanti.

Almost immediately, Mrs. Johnson noticed the natural ability Llanchie had for ballet. The feet positions and body extensions came effortlessly, matched with Llanchie's strong desire to excel and a propensity for discipline. Mrs. Johnson approached Llanchie's mother, singing praises, *"Mrs. Stevenson! Rosie is exceptionally talented!"* She saw Llanchie's potential for greatness and urged her to pursue a path that would surely lead to professional opportunities. To back up her claims, she offered a scholarship to the family for classes, removing any financial barrier that might have existed.

The studio became a second home for Llanchie, a close-knit community that provided love, support, and discipline. If a student had potential, Mrs. Johnson would require them to take all styles of dance offered. She also allowed them to teach classes for younger students. Llanchie frequented the studio multiple times a week; in her teenage years, she also taught classes. Mrs. Johnson would also readily find opportunities for the company to perform in events held in their local community. When cotillions and culturally based programs needed dancers, Mrs. Johnson's senior pro-class would dazzle the audiences with their talents. Over the years, Llanchie would become the center's outstanding star, landing the leading role in every performance.

Llanchie began gaining recognition for her talents outside of the dance studio; several local newspapers featured her and her dreams of a career in the ballet field. Her proud mother kept a scrapbook of every newspaper article she was in, starting from her teenage years until her retirement. She received accolades such as "Dancing Teenager of the Month" and "Most Promising Young Dancer." In 1961, her face appeared in Ebony Magazine after winning first place in a talent competition hosted by The Links Inc., one of the oldest national volunteer organizations. She was pictured accepting her award from the wife of the Governor of New York, Mr. Nelson Rockefeller.

Llanchie was easy-going but very shy; she allowed her talent to speak for her. Only her close family called her Llanchie;

her friends referred to her as Rosemarie. The delicate name matched the way she carried herself. Her closest friends were Lester Wilson and Marguerite DeLain, also fellow dancers from the Bernice Johnson Dance Studio. Lester was a few years older than they were; he drove a 1957 red and black Ford that enamored the young dancers. After rehearsals one night, the trio decided to take a joy ride around the city before heading to take Llanchie home. Unfamiliar with Llanchie's neighborhood in East Elmhurst, Lester got lost along the way. It was early morning when they finally made their way to her home. Her parents were understandably very angry with the group.

The High School of Performing Arts

When she approached the 9th grade, Llanchie faced the question of what educational avenue she should pursue. The high school where she and her neighborhood friends were zoned for held little interest to Llanchie. Witnessing her classmates' general lack of focus and the rising crime levels occurring around her school, she searched for an alternative. The choice seemed simple enough. On Manhattan's West 46th Street was the famous The High School of Performing Arts (PA), a public high school dedicated to young artists interested in honing their crafts. Until its merger with an art and music school and subsequent move, the likes of Al Pacino, Wesley Snipes, Eartha Kitt, Liza Minnelli, and Ben Vereen roamed the halls of this institution. The hit 1980s movie Fame was based on the lives of fictitious students who attended this school. She auditioned and earned a spot in the ballet department in 1958. Mrs.

Johnson was ecstatic, as Llanchie was the first from her studio to be accepted into this department. Her previous declaration regarding Llanchie's talent was confirmed.

Llanchie enjoyed her time at The High School of Performing Arts tremendously; unmistakable electric energy permeated the halls. Her friend Marguerite was accepted into the Modern dance department, and the two of them became inseparable. She stayed in the ballet department for her freshman year, taking dance classes in the morning, then switching to academics in the afternoon. During their lunch period, a live DJ would provide music; students would often freely dance along. Due to the nature of the school, Llanchie was able to take part in incredible opportunities such as making an appearance on the famed TV show American Bandstand and winning the dance competition with her partner. She knew she had to be the best amongst her peers. She vowed to jump higher, spin faster than her counterparts and leave no doubt about her rightful place at the school.

Removal from the Ballet Department

After having a positive freshman year, she was crestfallen when she learned that the school's administration switched her concentration from ballet to the Modern dance department. Instead of allowing her to develop her ballet talent, she was told that Modern dance was a better fit for her. This dance genre emerged in the early 20th century as a more relaxed offspring of the strict discipline nature of ballet. Overall her school lacked diversity; there were only six black students in Llanchie's graduating class. However, the Modern dance department had a slightly more diverse student body, unlike its ballet counterpart.

The argument was made that as a Black woman, Llanchie would be afforded better future employment opportunities in the world of Modern dance as opposed to the centuries-old, traditionally white world of ballet. *"She would look like a fly in a bowl of milk,"* the administration stated. They attempted to back their racist decision with claims that they were looking out for her future. Every child of color has moments in their lives when they are faced with the existing realities of racism. It is always constant in the background, often an unspoken truth needing little explanation. No level of talent, effort or discipline could overcome a path others chose for her because of the melanin-laced hue of her skin. She was honored and adored in previous enclaves of Blackness; now her excellence was cast aside simply because of the dominant society's notion of "just how the world works."

She was unable to hold back the fall of tears from this heartbreaking verdict. The passing of time seemed to slow down as she made the hour-long commute on the F train and connecting bus ride from Manhattan back to her home in Queens. Her first love was being stripped away; hours, months, and years of practice rendered irrelevant due to the percentage of brown in her pigmented skin. Her parents knew an upsetting event had unfolded the instant she entered their home. She poured out her disturbing news. *"I'll take care of it!"* Her father let her know immediately, and she believed him. Throughout the fourteen years of her young life, her parents never left her wanting anything. This situation would be no different. Herbert was quick to take action; he stormed up to the school the very next day and demanded to speak with the Program Director. Llanchie was not privy to the conversation, nor did she know the exact words her father used. However, she believes he threatens litigation in a calm but stern manner.

While it is unknown what happened between the director and Herbert, the results were favorable for Llanchie. She was allowed to rejoin the ballet department that same day, taking her rightful place amongst the other white ballerinas, many of which were remarkably less talented than she was. This incident cemented the idea that she could be the first African American to do many things. She always shares that her pioneering was not intentional; she simply desired to dance and pursue her white counterparts' path. While others might have cowered in fear of the opposition they would likely face, Llanchie had grit and used her talents to jeté over any obstacles in her way.

As she entered her final year of high school, Llanchie's parents had set their sights on The Juilliard School, the nation's premier higher education institution for performing arts. However, Llanchie was finished with the study of dance and was ready to forge a professional career. Thinking long term, she knew her body would only serve her for a limited number of years, given the wear and tear she put it through daily. She believed that college could wait; she had more significant stages to dance on and could not wait any longer to discover them.

In the summer of 1962, at the age of 17, Llanchie graduated and was awarded "Most Improved" by the ballet department. She felt that the administration was reluctant to give her this award, but she truly deserved it. She was disappointed that the school offered her a vocational diploma in the study of dance rather than a traditional high school diploma. She thought that perhaps she could prove that she should receive a different certificate by taking additional high school courses over the summer. However, she soon was distracted from any further study as she began the auditioning process for ballet companies.

3
DANCING PROFESSIONALLY

"From his roots as a slave, the American Negro - sometimes sorrowing, sometimes jubilant but always hopeful - has touched, illuminated, and influenced the most remote preserves of world civilization. I and my dance theater celebrate this trembling beauty." - Alvin Ailey

WITH HER HOPES set on joining a dance company, she began the treacherous process of auditioning. Whatever audition she could find, she gave her all in demonstrating her physical abilities. Despite her talent, she was not offered any paid opportunities. She traveled to Toronto in hopes of earning a spot in the National Ballet of Canada. At the end of the audition, the two directors walked around her speaking French. Assuming that a Black girl from America would not understand the foreign language, they freely shared their thoughts about her performance. *"What about her?"* One said in French, clearly recognizing her talent. *"I am not taking a black girl!"* the other director responded. Having studied French in high school, Llanchie immediately knew that she would not be hired and exactly why.

Llanchie took a job at Stacks, a specialty coin collection store in Manhattan. Her simple role initially was to hand-address envelopes for shipping. However, her supervisors admired her intelligence and work ethic, which led them they trained her to do bookkeeping. They also supported her continued pursuit of a dance career, arranged her schedule around auditions and ballet classes. Llanchie started paying for what lessons she could afford at the American Ballet Theatre to improve her skills. She recalls attending a class one day with two of the topic ballet dancers in the world at the time, Margot Fonteyn and Rudolf Nureyev. As the only Black dancer in attendance, she felt the burden of having to dance exceptionally well in their presence on behalf of her entire race.

The Alvin Ailey Dance Company

As she continued to audition, she heard about a newly established Modern dance company founded by an African American dancer and choreographer. Alvin Ailey entered the world of dance later than many after watching a show in his late teens. He began to study multiple styles of dance at a studio ran by dancer and choreographer Lester Horton. Horton's studio was one of the very few establishments in the 1940s that would offer training to dancers of all backgrounds. Alvin perfected his craft and eventually joined

Horton's dance company. However, after Horton's untimely death in 1953, Ailey assumed a leadership role in the company. Eventually, Ailey moved to New York and established his own company, the Alvin Ailey American Dance Theater, in 1958.

Eventually, Ailey moved to New York and established his own company, the Alvin Ailey American Dance Theater, in 1958. Ailey used the genre of modern dance to create dynamic performances highlighting and honoring the Black experience. His dance classes were rumored to be high-energy and tremendous fun. Llanchie was curious and enrolled in one taught by Alvin Ailey himself. Her balletic talents and skill immediately were noticeable, and she stood out to the teacher. Before the class ended, Alvin Ailey pointed his finger at her and declared, *"I want you for my company."*

Thus, she was offered her first professional dancing job at the age of 17 without an audition. She demonstrated her talent in the class, an audition unnecessary after Ailey witnessed her movements. She immediately began touring domestically with the company performing in major cities across the United States. As the youngest member traveling, Llanchie expected to be cuddled in the beginning. However, she soon realized she wanted to garner the respect of her company members as an adult. She remembers trying to style her hair and alter her appearance to appear more mature.

In August of 1963, the company participated in the Jacob's Pillow Dance Festival, the longest-running dance event of its kind. Llanchie took the stage for the song "House of the

Rising" with two other dancers and performed part of the company's signature piece, Revelations, where she danced to "Fix Me, Jesus" alongside James Truitte. In April 1964, The Los Angeles Times offered praise for the group's performance on UCLA's campus, *"In the matter of technique, one could not find better equipped dancers than...Rosemarie Stevenson."* (Arlen, 1964)

Her most memorable experience with the company also occurred in 1963 at an event called Century of Negro Progress Exposition. A hundred-year prior, then-President Abraham Lincoln declared the freedom of those enslaved Americans through the Emancipation Proclamation. The Exposition aimed to celebrate and remember this pivotal event in history. Famed composer and jazz musician Duke Ellington was tapped to curate a visual and audio exhibit. Alvin Ailey Dance Company and several other Black dance troupes brought his vision to life. Llanchie was one of the youngest dancers performing at this festival. She recalls Duke Ellington searching for a dancer to teach a curtesy to an individual who would present his orchestra. Llanchie offered to help, and he showed his gratitude later on by buying her dinner.

While she traveled as a member of the Alvin Ailey Dance Company, the founder continuously commented on what he believed should be her career trajectory. She would often hear from him: *"You're so talented in ballet," "You should really be trying to get into the ballet world," "You could become the first Black ballerina with your talent."* Alvin Ailey constantly urged her to try to break into the historically white-dominated society of professional ballet. While Raven Wilkinson had made history in 1955 as the first African-American ballerina to dance for a major American company, Llanchie's complexion would defy the colorism that often negatively impact darker-skinned Americans.

Even with a vigorous travel schedule, she was not allowed to take breaks like the other members of the company. When her fellow dancers would rest, she was lacing up her pointe shoes and practicing her fouettés, intricate fast-paced turns that are difficult to master but appear effortless when perfected. As she practiced to maintain her natural talent and skills, any observer would be in awe. She continuously got feedback that her destiny was beyond the modern dance company.

Radio City Music Hall

Once back in New York City, the idea was planted by her current company to audition for the Radio City Music Hall Corps de Ballet. The audition was a full-circle moment for Llanchie, having first been introduced to ballet in the majestic hall decades earlier. Since its inception in 1933, the members of this now-defunct company dazzled the stage to the audience's amazement. Gaining a position would make her the first African-American ballerina in this company. Little black girls in the future, admiring the ballerinas on the stage, would be able to see themselves represented, unlike what she had witnessed years ago.

At the time, Marc Platt served as the director of the company. He watched her every move as she spun, jumped, and danced with every part of her body and soul. Platt paused reflectively at the end of her audition. After a moment, he told her to practice her fouettés and come back in two weeks. It was not an immediate rejection, but Llanchie did not quite know what to make of this setback. She knew it was a common notion amongst dance teachers and directors that if a dancer could excel in the movement of fouettés, it was believed that she could do anything. Her parents nor the leadership at Alvin Ailey let this setback diminish her aspirations. While keeping up with the demands of the dance company she was currently a member of, she spent every spare moment practicing and practicing. Thinking back on those two weeks, she always says she was not even allowed a water break.

She returned weeks later to audition again. This time she received a positive answer from the director: "Yes, let's take her!" Llanchie was excited for the new direction and her role in pushing the envelope of equity in the world of dancing. All those in her circle celebrated this momentous accomplishment, from Alvin Ailey Dance Company members to her church community. Her former dance school was one of her biggest cheerleaders. While former students of the Bernice Johnson Dance studio had achieved success on Broadway and in theatre, Llanchie was unique in her accomplishments in the world of ballet.

A strong community of supporters and mentors had a significant influence on Llanchie. They saw the unique gift of ballet she had been given and would not let her waste these talents. From her first dance teacher, to a father that would not accept the status quo, to Alvin Ailey who would not allow her to lose her competitive edge, Llanchie was ushered into the world of dance knowing that she would command it. A supportive village of church members, dancers and extended family fought for her, celebrated her accomplishment, and lifted her in every possible way.

As a member of the Corps de Ballet, Llanchie would endure long hours. In the early mornings, the dancers would meet for rehearsal and to learn any new choreography. Afterward, she would perform four shows a day, with the final performance at 8 pm. A taxi at the end of the day returned her to her home in Queens. Often her cousin Candy would visit her in two-hour breaks between the show. Larger productions would also include the famous Rockettes, each dancer performing their respective movements, creating a grand performance. A taxi at the end of the day returned her to her home in Queens. Often her cousin Candy would visit her in two-hour breaks between the show. Larger productions would also include the famous Rockettes, each dancer performing their respective movements, creating a grand performance. A taxi at the end of the day returned her to her home in Queens. Often her cousin Candy would visit her in two-hour breaks between the show. Larger productions would also include the famous Rockettes, each dancer performing their respective movements, creating a grand performance. Some of the dances were easy to execute, such as the renowned production of Balero. The biggest challenge for all of the Corps was that the dancers were attached to strings to immediate marionettes. If the steps were not precise, a dancer could get tangled with her fellow Corps member.

Even though the grueling schedule, Llanchie enjoyed doing what she loved. Llanchie found a kindred spirit in another dancer named Jo Rowan, and their close friendship made the long days. There were unique challenges Llanchie faced as the only African-American dancer. When she received her stage outfits from the costume department, she would have to alter the clothing to match her skin tone. Often she would dye the elastic straps so that she would have the same strapless appears as the other dancers.

4

CLASSICAL TRAINING

"God creates, I do not create. I assemble and I steal everywhere to do it - from what I see, from what the dancers can do, from what others do." - George Balanchine

WHILE THE NATION grappled with the repercussion of the Vietnam War and issues of racial equality in the mid-1960s, Llanchie tried to make a name for herself. She worked as a dancer at the Radio City Music Hall for two years. Once the excitement and newness wore off, she began to assess her career compared to other ballerinas with whom she interacted. Her dissatisfaction continued to grow when other ballet dancers came to Radio City Music Hall to perform in particular. While she was fulfilling her dreams of dancing professionally, she knew she was missing something by not holding a position in a traditional touring ballet company. Instinctively, she knew that she was limiting herself and needed to find a way to step into more significant challenges.

School of American Ballet

Llanchie set her sights on the premiere school for ballet in the country. The best of the best was the School of American Ballet (SAB) and its associated company, the New York City Ballet, both founded by choreographer George Balanchine. Considered the greatest and most influential American choreographer of ballet by most members of the dance world, Balanchine is often referenced as the father of American ballet.

Similar to the requirements of admission into The High School of Performing Arts, Llanchie's enrollment was predicated on an audition. The School of American Ballet touts itself as being highly selective with steep tuition prices, often an additional barrier to prospective students. Nevertheless, Llanchie's talent would again prove to open doors for her. She was not only granted admission but also received a scholarship to hone her abilities. Hard work was never an issue for her, and she remained at the school for the next two years. She understood this unique privilege, not only as an African-American but also given the selective nature of the school. She was determined in every moment to outperform her peers in any way she could. The total scholarship was not the only support she received. Other ballerinas would give her their older pointe shoes, cutting down expenses she would need to pay. She worked part-time at odd jobs to make ends meet, never shying away from doing what she needed to do to pursue her dreams and survive. She was confident that an offer for a role in the company was imminent as many of her classmates began shifting to paid positions.

Yet a job offers never came. Her dream to become a member of the famed New York City Ballet company slowly faded as the weeks and months passed. Attempting to understand the situation better, she finally sought guidance from Diana Adams, one of the school's directors. She had a simple request, an inquiry to Mr. Balanchine regarding her prospects of joining the company. The director returned with disappointing news; the feedback was that a Black woman would disrupt the optics of uniformity or literally "break the corps line." Balanchine was not ready to make that type of history. In his mind, he already had one Black male dancer but was not prepared to accept a ballerina in the ranks of his white female dancers. He was toying with the idea of a separate corps de ballet with only Black ballerinas. However, Llanchie saw this idea for what it was; a stalling tactic and a lack of respect for the talent she was bringing forth.

Coming to the end of her scholarship, she would have to pay to continue training with Balanchine. She was disillusioned and disheartened, but the Director encouraged her not to abandon her dreams of working for a ballet company and suggested she look into the Joffrey Ballet Company, based in New York. Her talents again led her to a scholarship, and she continued to hope the right opportunity would come along. As she trained, she worked as a dancer anywhere she could, continuing at Radio City Music Hall and the Alvin Ailey Dance Company.

In 1966, Llanchie was approached by Arthur Mitchell, an African-American principal ballet dancer for the New York

City Ballet company. United Nations Educational, Scientific, and Cultural Organization (UNESCO) was sponsoring an international event, the First World Festival of Negro Arts. Mitchell was appointed to assemble a company consisting of talented dancers to represent the United States. Llanchie, along with 21 other dancers, was selected to travel and perform in Dakar, Senegal. Although they were not compensated for their efforts, the dancers hoped the festival would lead to greater opportunities. Unfortunately, funding to support the group's participation was drastically cut, and future plans to establish a company were abandoned.

Jones-Haywood Ballet School & Capitol Ballet

She also ventured out to a few other small, local companies for seasonal work. She performed for Brooklyn Ballet Company and was a soloist in Garden State Ballet's annual Nutcracker performance. Determined to forge a path for herself, she traveled by bus on weekends to Washington, D.C. to dance with the only Black ballet company in existence at the time, Capitol Ballet. This small racially integrated company was a separate arm of the Jones-Haywood Dance School, a ballet school in the nation's capital. Doris W. Jones had faced the barrier of segregation when trying to learn ballet as schools would refuse to allow her to take classes. After meeting Clarie Haywood at a summer camp, Mrs. Jones persuaded Haywood to open a ballet school in 1941 in the nation's capital. The school aimed to offer training to any child desiring to learn no matter their race. Arthur Mitchell often was a guest instructor during breaks from dancing with New York City Ballet.

Their school was well-known and respected for producing highly qualified Black ballet dancers. In 1961, Jones and Haywood launched a professional company called Capitol Ballet. It was one of the first predominately African-American ballet companies in the United States, with Jones serving as the artistic director. The company faced numerous challenges as the two women attempted to expand their reach. Funding to support their vision was often a struggle, and grants for the arts were minimal. However, Jones and Haywood were determined and coordinated several shows that would often featuring guest performers from other companies. Llanchie would lend her talents when she could, dancing in several performances in the local metropolitan area. Many of their shows were held in Cramton Auditorium on the campus of Howard University.

National Ballet of Washington

While New York and California were considered the premier locations for ballet, other cities began making their mark in the dance world. In 1944, the Washington School of Ballet opened its doors for ballet instruction. The school started completing domestic tours, and eventually, advanced students held performances. An official company would later be incorporated in the mid-70s, but during the 60s, there was a vacancy of a professional dance company in Washington, D.C. Perhaps seeing this gap but unable to convince the leadership of his vision, the co-director of Washington School of Ballet at the time decided to branch out and create his own company.

Frederic Franklin co-founded the National Ballet of Washington in 1962, and he was looking for dancers to join their corps. Llanchie was hopeful, as the company had already hired a Black male dancer. In retrospect, Llanchie wonders if there was pressure from a national sponsor to have a Black dancer that incentivizes the founder's desire to diversify their company. Fredrick Franklin reached out to Doris Jones, the director of Capitol Dance Company, to help them search for a Black ballerina. While there was incredible talent at the Jones-Haywood Ballet School, including rising star Sandra Green, Mrs. Jones suggested Llanchie, who danced periodically with her company.

Llanchie was instructed to lie about her age when she went to audition. Mrs. Jones believed that if they knew she was 21 years old, they would not accept her thinking she was past her prime. Llanchie auditioned for the co-founder, and she was hired immediately as the first African-American female dancer. While the features on the company's Black male dancer made him somewhat racially ambiguous, there would be no doubt of her ethnicity given the depth of melanin in her skin.

The vision of Frederic Franklin was to share the art of ballet with all Americans, not just those living in the Washington Metropolitan area. He wanted to gain a nationwide reach. This would be accomplished by constant travel to as many cities as they could across America. Llanchie found herself dancing on small stages in Kansas and Texas and larger venues such as the Grand Ole Opry in Nashville, Tennessee. Llanchie enjoyed her time practicing and performing with the National Ballet of Washington. The company could not afford to pay the dancers outside of the dance season, so she collected unemployment during these periods. The time in

Washington, D.C. was her first experience living independently away from her parents. She was incredibly lonely and would frequently keep her television on just to add background noise to her quiet apartment.

As her schedule allowed, Llanchie would also participate as a guest performer with Capitol Ballet Company when she could. Llanchie held Mrs. Jones in high regard for recommending her to the National Ballet of Washington and admired her impact on cultivating talented Black ballerinas. One of the most memorable shows was a special tribute held to honor Dr. Martin Luther King Jr. after his assassination. Using her gift of movement, she hoped to help the nation in the aftermath of this horrific tragedy.

She was close with one dancer, Jane Miller, a soloist who trained alongside Llanchie at the School of America Ballet. During the Christmas season, the company offers a performance of Peter Ilyich Tchaikovsky's "Nutcracker." Jane Miller was the featured soloist in the Arabian Dance. To create the aesthetic of an individual from a foreign land, she would use makeup to darken her skin. After growing tired of the cumbersome process of heavy makeup, she mentioned to the director that Llanchie looked more the part and suggested that Llanchie be featured in this solo role. Franklin agreed, and Llanchie was excited to own the spotlight.

5
CREATING A LEGACY

"You must believe in what you're doing and, against all odds...stick to it." - Arthur Mitchell

IN 1967, Llanchie traveled the country with the National Ballet of Washington and danced in numerous performances for primarily white audiences. The Civil Rights Movement had won some significant battles with the passing of the Civil Rights Act of 1964, outlawing racial discrimination. Despite this and other laws restoring rights, much more work still was needed. Protests and riots sprung up in major cities across the country during 1967 and 1968. Society as a whole was reexamining systemic injustices, and deficiencies were becoming more apparent to many Americans.

Race Relations

. . .

In the backdrop of nationwide discord, classical music and balletic movement offered viewers a momentary break from the harsh realities occurring around them in their beloved country. Llanchie was not afforded the luxury of complete emergence into the glamorous but fictitious dance world. While traveling to over a hundred U.S. towns and cities, the company decided several times not to have her step on stage, fearing the backlash. Spartanburg, South Carolina, and Montgomery, Alabama were among the cities where she was forced to sit in the audience and watch her fellow company members perform.

Sitting alone in a crowd during performances had a profound impact on Llanchie. While her race had shaped her career in unique ways before this, she was experiencing the deep racism of the South firsthand. Her race was deemed problematic in other areas as well. Artistic directors would tell her, "Well...we don't know where to put you," using the excuse of historical accuracy to deny her participation in specific productions. Her contributions would be relegated to fantasy ballets like the Nutcracker, with some creative license due to the fictional setting. Factors of race would not corrupt the storyline for inanimate objects such as snowflakes.

The assassination of Dr. Martin Luther King Jr. that occurred on the evening of April 4 of 1968 shook the entire nation in profound ways. The single deadly gunshot that entered his right cheek penetrated the hearts and minds of Americans from different walks of life. A powerful life cut short forced many to examine the issues he had put his voice behind for years, compelling many to create change in areas of their control.

. . .

Dance Theatre of Harlem

The dance world was not immune to the ripple effect of Dr. King's death. Arthur Mitchell was especially moved to action by the horrific event. He had earned a position of elite privilege in the New York City Ballet, allowing him to successfully navigate the company that had denied Llanchie a job years prior. Specialized roles were created to highlight his talents yet still create digestible performances for audience members unwilling to view African-Americans as equals. This luxury could not be replicated for every person of color with talent. Wanting to use dance as a mechanism to create social change, Mitchell sprouted an idea to simultaneously launch a school and a company that would allow for greater diversity in the ballet world. Naturally, he reached out to Llanchie due to their shared training under George Balanchine and her work as a professional ballerina.

Llanchie was intrigued with the idea of a Black company and supported the efforts of Mitchell while on summer break from the National Ballet of Washington. Joined by three other Black dancers aiming to push the dance world forward, Llanchie was critical in the school and company's inception. Initially, both were housed as the Dance department in the Harlem School of the Arts. One of the first outreach efforts by the newly established company was a lecture demonstration in Rensselaerville, a small town outside of New York City. The request for the program came to Arthur Mitchell very early on in the founding of the school and company, giving the dancers little time to prepare for their debut. The performance was kept relatively simple; Llanchie danced with the three members of the company, Walter Raines, Lydia Abarca, and Gerald Banks. Raines, who danced the pas de deux with Llanchie, describes in a later interview, *"By no stretch of the imagination could one have called this a good performance... it was the reaction of the people after we had finished that struck me. It was the look on their faces – expressing that they had just witnessed one of the most beautiful things that they had ever seen in their lives."* (Latham, 1973)

To garner publicity for their efforts, the company hosted numerous educational demonstrations to introduce ballet to young children. Additionally, the weekly rehearsals on Wednesdays were open to the public, which allowed for the attendance of prominent dance community members. As the fledgling company attempted to get off the ground, Llanchie grew impatient, witnessing a lack of professionalism to which she had grown accustomed. Conflict arose between the founder and director of the Harlem School of the Arts and Arthur Mitchell, eventually leading Mitchell to establish a separate ballet company. She returned to National Ballet of Washington for a second year but kept abreast of Mitchell's inroads to solidify his company. The company was incorporated in February of 1969 with famous individuals taking place as members of the board of directors, including choreographer George Balanchine, actress Cicely Tyson and actor Brock Peters. Llanchie would lend her talent occasionally throughout the spring of 1969 until she officially joined the company as a founding member and principal ballerina.

Principal and Founding Dancer

. . .

Unlike her time at Alvin Ailey, Llanchie was now one of the more seasoned members of the company. Virginia Johnson, who later became the artistic director for the Dance Theatre of Harlem, stated in an interview, *"And there was Llanchie Stevenson, a wonderful dancer who had performed with the National Ballet in Washington. She was the real professional in the group. The rest of us were just kids."* (Harss, 2013) Llanchie would often confess to her early skepticism but found Mitchell to continue challenging her to grow as a ballerina. While the salary was modest, she loved being back in New York City and occupying the stage in the full manifestation of her Blackness.

The Ford Foundation provided a $315,000 grant, which gave Arthur Mitchell the ability to start to accomplish the goals he had outlined for his school and company. Additionally, Mitchell secured funding through New York State Council and the National Endowments for the Arts despite the regulations that a company needed to be in operation for over five years to receive funding. Llanchie began touring again domestically with The Dance Theatre of Harlem. Audiences of all backgrounds witnessed the incredible skill of the racially diverse dancers. While there were multiple obstacles to overcome, the company experienced success almost immediately. Because of his close relationship with Balanchine, Mitchell was given the rights to several notable dances Balanchine had choreographed, providing much-needed legitimacy to his new company. There was also a hunger for Black excellence that Llanchie and the other professional dancers satisfied--the dynamic spirit of the company astounded every viewer.

The Dance Theatre of Harlem was a revolutionary concept. It was often unthinkable for persons of color to take up the balletic tradition and excel in it. The common prejudice was that Black bodies could not perform in the athletic but graceful nature ballet requires. There is also the idea of keeping the historical authenticity of the dances created in the 1700s. It was seemingly unthinkable that any persons of color would exist as essential characters during this timeframe. In 1970, the company traveled to the Caribbean for its first international performance in the Bahamas, Curaçao, Trinidad, and Jamaica. Llanchie was treated with special reverence due to her Aruban and Trinidadian roots. The company made its first European tour during the following summer, beginning in Italy and traveling to Amsterdam and Belgium. In August of 1970, Llanchie returned to Jacob's Pillow to perform in its ninth week of the festival. She took the stage performing the evening shows, dancing the Pas de deux in Holbert Suite. The company received rave reviews, many critics commenting on how quickly the company achieved success and produced high-quality performances.

For Llanchie, being a part of Mitchell's company was the realization of her childhood dreams. She enjoyed the ability to display her talents alongside other excellent dancers. As a principal ballerina, she was able to take center stage and contributed to advocate for diversity in the ballet world. As the years progressed, newspapers reviewing the Dance Theatre of Harlem would offer the highest praise for Llanchie. An article in the Sacramento Bee wrote, *"...and later there were some beautiful dance phrases from a girl with the right springs in all the right muscles, Llanchie Stevenson, who might just be the best dancer in the troupe"* (Glackin, 1971). She was featured in the Sunday edition of The Washington Star regarding her transition from the National Ballet of Washington (Warren, 1970).

. . .

Skin-colored Tights

One day in rehearsal, something she had been looking at for years stood out in a distinctive way. Since the age of eight, she had been wearing pink tights, the standard uniform for dancers of all ages. Nevertheless, in that moment, the stark contrast between her beautiful dark brown arms and the white of her tights was disfiguring. The light pink tights and pointe shoes reflected the flesh tone of the creators of the art form and centuries of its performers. The tradition of the pink color predated Llanchie for over 300 years and had never been questioned on its applicability to dancers of different backgrounds.

Llanchie began to feel disjointed, unable to abandon the notion that pink legs and soft brown arms were subtly diminishing the grace and power of her movement. In an act of rebellion, she came up with a simple solution. She began wearing brown tights over her pink tights allowing for an uninterrupted look from head to toe. Mitchell immediately noticed of how this completely changed the aesthetic of the dancer's body and ordered all the company members to follow suit for an upcoming performance.

Soon, the company also had the ballerinas dye their pointe shoes to match their unique skin tone to complete the uniform look. It was quite an undertaking, but the final product completely transformed the look of an entire production. This slight but significant change debuted on stage in later years and became a signature feature of the company. Llanchie's innovation sprouted a subtle change.

This slight adjustment to the dancers' costumes set the Dance Theatre of Harlem apart as a unique company that wholeheartedly embraced diversity and highlighted the efforts it would take to feature the talents of its dancers in the best possible ways.

Llanchie paved the way for a revolutionary shift in the dance world, although it is still not universally accepted nearly 50 years later. Lauren Anderson, American's first Black principal dancer; Misty Copeland, American Ballet Theatre's first black principal dancer; and Michaela De Prince, soloist for the Dutch National Ballet, have performed in colored tights. Recently, a commercial for Amazon showcased an African-American ballerina and featured her wearing tights matching her skin tone during her final performance. Dancers globally are embracing tights and shoes that match the natural glow of melanin in their skin.

6

GUIDED BY FAITH

"The most productive force in our lives is the sensible regard for the Creator, the Lord Creator who has power and authority over all things." - Imam Warith D. Mohammed

LLANCHIE PAVED the way for a revolutionary shift in the dance world, although it is still not universally accepted nearly 50 years later. Lauren Anderson, American's first Black principal dancer; Misty Copeland, American Ballet Theatre's first black principal dancer; and Michaela De Prince, soloist for the Dutch National Ballet have performed in colored tights. Recently, a commercial for Amazon showcased an African-American ballerina and featured her wearing tights matching her skin tone during her final performance. Dancers globally are embracing tights and shoes that match the natural glow of melanin in their skin.

Furthermore, Llanchie began to feel that there was a noticeable trend of favoritism within the company.

Although she believed her experience and talent would speak for themselves, she continued to witness star roles being offered to other dancers. She had her sights on the pas-de-deux in the famed dance "Agon," a classical ballet choreographed by George Balanchine, which would feature a male and female soloist. However, she was never given the role. She speculated on the reasoning for this treatment, wondering if the root cause was her departure from the company during the initial stages of the development. She had returned to dance primarily for the National Ballet of Washington while other loyalists of Arthur Mitchell's vision stayed.

Another theory she developed was that the bias could be due to her weight. Dancers were constantly comparing and contrasting their physique, and she could not help but compare her body to others. Members with less muscular figures and thinner structures seemed to be preferred by Arthur Mitchell. She tried numerous diets, but her already slim body was resistant to any weight loss. She even hoped that her wearing flesh-colored tights would give an illusion of a leaner frame.

Feeding her Soul

In the fall of 1971, the Dance Theatre of Harlem secured a permanent location, an old garage and warehouse, and renovated it to meet the needs of an emerging dance company and school. Llanchie would take a bus to work and dismount at a busy street corner. Every day she would pass a Nation of Islam clothing store where the organization's women could purchase custom-tailored long jacket style dresses and wide-legged pants.

In the early 1930s, an individual claiming the name Fard Muhammad established a political-religious organization in Detriot, Michigan. Called The Nation of Islam, Fard Muhammad instructed his followers to shift their mindset from integrating with those who have historically rejected Blacks. America's long history of the subhuman treatment of African-Americans left many searching for solutions for establishing equity and true freedom. The Nation of Islam offered a unique answer to society's racial issues that resonated with many. The religion of Islam, followed by billions across the world, was used as a foundation to establish a mental shift in the followers. To address economic disparities, the Nation of Islam prided itself on creating infrastructures that would support total independence from the American society. All of the amenities of a sovereign state were developed, including businesses, schools, and community centers. After its leader Fard Muhammad disappeared under mysterious circumstances, one of Fard's pupils, Elijah Poole, eventually assumed complete control of the organization in 1946. Called the Honorable Elijah Muhammad by his followers, Muhammad continued to expand the political and religious message of the Nation of Islam.

Llanchie was vaguely aware of the Nation of Islam but had not given the organization much thought when she would see its male members on street corners selling newspapers or selling bean pies. However, the signature uniforms in bright pastels hung in the shop's window often caught Llanchie's eyes on her daily commute. One day, her eyes landed on a book in the window display titled "How to Eat to Live," written by Elijah Muhammad. As she was constantly exploring diets to address her challenges in the company, she thought this might provide a solution. She devoured the book, her appetite for knowledge consuming her waking moments. Llanchie immediately began eating only one meal a day, which was the recommended practice:

> "Do not eat too much of anything - good or bad food - and do not eat but once a day. You will soon tell me how much better you feel." (Muhammad, 1967)

She quickly shed ten pounds from her already small figure. Although those around her immediately noticed the results, the weight loss had little effect in landing the roles she was trying to achieve. However, a subtle shift had begun to occur as she decided to look more into the teachings of the man who gave her physical success on the scale. Perhaps his words could render peace for her soul and fill her emotionally and spiritually. Dissatisfied with the Methodist church she grew up in, Llanchie attended worship services of different Christian denominations hoping for a connection.

Every Sunday, Llanchie would visit the homes of friends that were outside of the dance world. One of her friends had matriculated into the Nation of Islam and appeared to have the type of life Llanchie wanted for herself. Llanchie admired the internal peace and joy she could see radiating from her friend as she tended to her young children and loving husband. Approaching her late 20s, society at the time dictated that Llanchie was past due to start a family and have children of her own.

The Nation of Islam

She decided to attend her first meeting of the Nation of Islam; sisters dressed in bright pastel clothing greeted her warmly as she stepped into the temple. Immediately she felt like she had entered into a different world with unfamiliar cultural expectations and norms. Men and women sat separately, and lectures integrated Arabic words into the lessons presented. The members were ordered to follow a very disciplined life that emphasized unique daily practices and rituals. As an only child, she loved being embraced by the community of sisters eager to guide her.

Her first meeting led to many more. Slowly she began adopting the traditions of the Nation of Islam and applied to join the organization. She sent a letter to the headquarters in Chicago stating her intention and patiently waited for her acceptance as she gradually embraced a new lifestyle. Her fellow dancers noticed the shuttle shift in her but encouraged her. She humorously recalls one dancer stopping her when she was about to consume a slice of pepperoni pizza, educating her on the origins of the topping. Her way of dressing shifted as she opted to cover her head with a small scarf and wear loose-fitting clothing, even to her dance practices. A newspaper in Iowa reporting on the company's visit to the states snapped a photo of her wearing a scarf covering her hair alongside Arthur Mitchell and other company members. During her performances, she stopped wear making up on stage.

After a performance in Delaware, she met up with her cousin Candy, who was initially shocked to see her in modest attire. Candy commented that she believed Llanchie had a remarkable life traveling and performing. She could not understand why Llanchie would consider giving it up, especially how hard she had worked to get where she was. Llanchie responded that Candy's chosen profession as a teacher inspired her, and she thought Candy's life was more admirable than hers. While her father was relatively ambivalent about her pending conversion, her mother was horrified. Llanchie was leaving the Methodist tradition she had been raised in to join a religion unknown to Ruby. Her mother started visiting Christian churches of different denominations praying for her daughter's salvation. As she kneeled in the pews of each, she prayed that her daughter would accept their doctrine over the foreign religion of Islam.

A New Faith

Alas, Ruby's prayers went unanswered as Llanchie received her official acceptance into the Nation of Islam. She discarded her last name and replaced it with a single letter X. Numbers were also given to distinguish the temple members, but Llanchie's name was unique. With a desire to keep in line with the organization's rules, she wrote a letter to the Honorable Elijah Muhammad asking for his wisdom on her dancing career. She received a response from him that Muslim women were not allowed to dance in front of men. Additionally, the costumes of most performances did not fit in the dress code of her new faith.

With this decree came Llanchie's decision to retire from ballet after completing the final performances she was contractually obligated to do. There was tremendous disappointment among those who knew and loved Llanchie. The general feeling was that she still had so much to give the dance world of dance as a Black ballerina. Nevertheless, Llanchie had found something that spoke to her soul. The Muslim faith profoundly resonated with her, and she enjoyed growing her knowledge and understanding of the religion. While she refrained from participating in any performances after her conversion, ballet remains an integral part of her life. She taught ballet to children in several ballet schools. Several of her former students remark that she was the only dance teacher that gave written exams as part of her classes. She organized classes for numerous years to introduce young Muslim girls to the art form as a means of exercise.

By the fall of 1972, she was fully immersed into her new life, even taking a job in the same store where she had first purchased the book "How to Eat to Live." She attended Arabic, cooking, and sewing classes every Saturday through the Muslim Girls Training (MGT) program. Due to the competitive nature of the ballet world, she had never developed healthy, meaningful relationships within the different dance companies in which she worked. Once in the Nation, the feelings of sisterhood were undeniable and authentic.

The mission of the Nation of Islam allowed her to feel a part of something bigger than herself and connect with others in a unique sorority of faithful believers. She felt as if a separate nation within America was being formed, and she had pledged complete allegiance along with thousands of other women. Having always been keen on discipline, she believed her soul had reconnected with its natural inclination as a Muslim. Llanchie not only found an awakening of her spirituality, but an all-inclusive way of thinking and being that uplifted not only herself as a Black woman but also had the potential to transform the entire African-American community.

7

LIFE AFTER BALLET

"I think when you begin to think of yourself as having achieved something, then there's nothing left for you to work towards. I want to believe that there is a mountain so high that I will spend my entire life striving to reach the top of it." - Cicely Tyson

BEFORE LEAVING the Dance Theatre of Harlem, Llanchie was at practice one day when a well-groomed gentleman stepped into the premises. Llanchie casually asked a fellow dancer, *"Who is that?"* as she watched him observe the end of rehearsal. She was told that he would be working as an academic coordinator for the company members who were still in high school. He would serve as a liaison between the company and the Professional Children's School, where they attended classes. This private school in Manhattan was geared towards young performers who were working and needed to complete state-mandated education requirements. Llanchie's immediate thought was that he was the type of man her parents would want her to marry. Llanchie's interest was piqued by their similar backgrounds from the Caribbean and his advanced degrees from Columbia Law.

Llanchie was distracted as her religious beliefs intensified and her commitment to ballet dancing was waning. Still, a tentative friendship was formed between this man named Mario Landa and Llanchie. Mario had taken a leave of absence from his corporate job at IBM at the time. He accompanied the Dance Theatre of Harlem on several tours during the winter months. The two spent increasing amounts of time in each other's company, even taking a memorable stroll together along the beach in the U.S. Virgin Islands.

However, no amount of charm could pull her from the path she had chosen, away from dancing and towards the faith-based movement. Once a full member, she let him know there would be no future for them as she could only marry a member of the Nation of Islam. The allegiance to her faith was stronger than the feelings she was developing. Llanchie was unwavering in her conviction, choosing her spiritual path over the prospects of marriage. She left behind thoughts of this man and his journey until fate placed them together on a plane heading to a Nation of Islam gathering in Chicago. It seemed the universe had brought them back together. Llanchie's parting words had inspired Mario to search for answers in the Nation of Islam as well.

Marriage and Motherhood

. . .

She began an official courtship with Mario 7X, who proposed to Llanchie with a simple, *"I think we should get married,"* stated while on a drive. It was under the ideology of the Nation of Islam that Mario 7X and Llanchie X wed on Saturday, April 7th, 1973. The foundation of their marriage was the teachings of The Nation of Islam. While they faced typical struggles of two adults in their late 20s trying to merge their separate lives into one, they would unite on the mission and principles put forward by this organization. The birth of their first child came less than a year later, in February 1974. Llanchie labored naturally for 18 hours at Harlem Hospital Center and delivered a beautiful baby girl whom they named Maryam 17X. Overjoyed by this new chapter of her life, Llanchie opted to stay home to care for her young daughter, as was the common practice of the women in the Nation of Islam.

1975 was a pivotal year marked by the sudden death of the Honorable Elijah Muhamad, the Nation of Islam leader. Warith Deen, his seventh son from his marriage to Sr. Clara, rose as the obvious choice to assume leadership, speaking to the community directly the day after the passing of his father. Over the next few years, Warith Deen would discredit the ideological beliefs of his father and usher those who remained in the organization toward the traditional practices of Islam observed by Muslims worldwide. He preached unity amongst all people and encouraged his followers to embrace parts of the dominant culture of America that were not in direct conflict with the teachings of Islam.

As they navigated their transition into the religion of Islam, the couple welcomed their first son, Malachi, in December of 1975. Because of his birth in this focal year, Llanchie X and

Mario 7X received permission from the organization to take an official holy last name, either Muhammad or Ahmad. They chose Ahmad, which means "worthy of praise." Eventually, Llanchie X adopted the first name Aminah, officially ending the legacy of a ballerina named Llanchie Stevenson.

Homeschooling

In the early 1980s, Llanchie and Mario relocated to the Washington D.C. metro area. Unlike her previous time in the nation's capital, she was now surrounded by her growing family. She focused the next two decades of her life on raising six children: three girls, Maryam Sara, Mina, and Majeedah, along with three boys, Malachi Abdul-Malik, Mujahid, and Mateen. Llanchie taught all of them the basics of ballet, believing it to be an excellent form of exercise. Her artistic talents seem to have transferred to several of her children; Abdul-Malik has become a well-known rapper and martial artist. Her son Mateen enjoys acro gymnastics and break dancing, while her daughter Majeedah was gifted with a beautiful singing voice.

To ensure proper spiritual and educational development, she homeschooled all of her children for most of their primary and secondary education. She approached her role as a teacher with the same discipline she applied to succeed in her dance career. Every aspect of the educational day was well planned and thought out. To keep six children organized, she set up the den in their home like a classroom. Desks and chairs in the middle of the room faced her teacher's desk; educational posters and chalkboards lined the walls.

The concern of legal action for choosing homeschooling was always on the back of the minds of Llanchie and Mario. In 1984, criminal charges of violating state education laws were brought against a Maryland couple who homeschooled their two children. This case pushed the conversation of homeschooling forward, causing legislation to regulate and guide this growing subculture.

Llanchie and Mario grew concerned that the legitimacy of their education efforts would also be questioned. To mitigate this risk, they obtained the curriculum offered in public schools and purchased textbooks from the same companies. In addition to the textbooks, Llanchie ordered the teacher's edition, which provided sample quizzes, tests, and other resources. Llanchie's cousin Candy, a school principal, would routinely administer standardized testing to ensure appropriate progression in their education. Additionally, the children would take the Secondary School Admission Test (SSAT) annually to monitor their learning compared to national averages. They routinely scored exceptionally well on these exams. When her older child reached higher grades, she would search for tutors to help Maryam with advanced subjects. Llanchie would sit and learn the materials to teach them to the rest of her children. This speaks to the sacrifice and forward-thinking she had in the pursuit of educating her children. Due to her dedication, four of her children graduated with undergraduate degrees, and two have obtained Master's degrees.

After her last child finished his schooling, she began a second career teaching various subjects, including physical education at a local Muslim school. She considers herself a lifelong learner, taking many college-level courses in her spare time. She has developed a passion for studying the Quran, the holy book of the Islamic faith. She copied the entire Arabic text of the book and is currently working towards memorizing all of its chapters.

Llanchie looks back on her ballet career fondly. She dreamt of being a famous ballerina when she was young. Although she did not reach the height of fame she thought she wanted, Llanchie feels blessed to have left a lasting mark on the dance world through her innovation of wearing tights that match a dancer's skin. Through the legacy of Llanchie Stevenson, ballet dancers of all shades, especially little Black girls and boys, are able to celebrate their beautiful skin as they wear skin-colored tights.

TIMELINE

- **1300s** – The art form of ballet emerges in France and Italy amongst societies' royalty and elite.
- **1661** – The first ballet school, the Academie Royale de Danse, opens in France.
- **1934** – The School of American Ballet was founded in New York City by George Balanchine.
- **1945** – Rosemarie "Llanchie" Stevenson was born in San Nicholas, Aruba.
- **1951** – Llanchie immigrated to the United States with her mother, Ruby.
- **1958** – Llanchie begins secondary school at The High School of Performing Arts. Alvin Ailey American Dance Theater, a modern dance company, was founded.
- **1961** – Doris Jones and Joan Haywood establish Capitol Ballet Company.
- **1962** – Llanchie graduates from high school and joins the Alvin Ailey American Dance Theater as a modern dancer.
- **1963** – Llanchie joins the Radio City Music Hall

Ballet Company as its first African-American dancer.
- **1964** – Llanchie begins studying at the School of American Ballet under George Balanchine.
- **1967** – Llanchie joins the National Ballet of Washington and the first African-American female member of their corps de ballet.
- **1968** – Dr. Martin Luther King Jr. was assassinated.
- **1969** – The Dance Theatre of Harlem is established and Llanchie joins Dance Theatre of Harlem, but continues to dance with the National Ballet of Washington.
- **1970** – Llanchie officially joins the Dance Theatre of Harlem as a founding member and principal dancer. She pioneers wearing colored tights.
- **1971** – Llanchie joins the Nation of Islam and retires from dancing.
- **1973** – Llanchie marries Mario Landa (Ahmad).
- **1975** – Llanchie transitions into the traditional Islam, which is practiced worldwide by over a billion believers.

KEY FIGURES

Alvin Ailey (1931-1989) – Ailey was an African-American dancer and choreographer who founded Alvin Ailey American Dance Theater. The style of dance featured in this company mixes jazz, modern, and other traditions to produce unique contemporary performances.

George Balanchine (1904-1983) – Known as the father of American ballet, Balanchine co-founded the School of American Ballet and the New York City Ballet. He is considered one of the most influential choreographers due to his distinctive style and influence on establishing the art of ballet in America.

Frederic Franklin (1914-2013) – Franklin was an English ballet dancer and choreographer. He co-directed the Washington Ballet and later co-founded the National Ballet of Washington, D.C.

Arthur Mitchell (1934-2018) – Mitchell was the first African-American male to become a principal dancer in a major ballet company. He performed with the New York City

Key Figures

Ballet company and later founded the Dance Theatre of Harlem.

Elijah Muhammad (1897-1975) – Muhammad rose to become the leader of the Nation of Islam, a faith-based organization with ties to Islam and Black Nationalism.

Warith Deen Muhammad (1933- 2008) – As the son of Elijah Muhammad, Warith inherited the leadership of the Nation of Islam from his father. He is responsible for the mass conversion of the followers of the Nation of Islam into mainstream practice of Islam.

Brock Peters (1927-2005) – Peters was an African-American actor best known for his roles on Star Trek and movies such as To Kill a Mockingbird (1962). He served as the chairman of the board when the Dance Theatre of Harlem was established.

Marc Platt (1913–2014) – Platt was an American dancer and actor. He directed the Radio City Music Hall ballet company for numerous years.

Cicely Tyson (1924- 2021) – Tyson was an award-winning African-American actress and recipient of the Presidential Medal of Freedom. As a close friend of Arthur Mitchell, she was actively involved in the Dance Theatre of Harlem from its inception.

BIBLIOGRAPHY

Arlen, W. (1964, April 14). Ailey Dancers Please in Program at UCLA. *Los Angeles Times*, p. 25.

Barnes, C. (1971, January 3). A Best (Not 10) List for 1970. *New York Times*, p. D11

Battey, J. (1964, June). Dancers in Capitol Ballet Display Uneven Ability. *The Washington Post*.

Battey, J. (1968, May 30). Dancers Pay Tribute to King. *The Washington Post, Times Herald*.

Bellamy, C. (1971, Feb 11). Black Ballet is Beautiful. *Bay State Banner*.

Budducke, M. (1972, January 23). Rhythm and Splendor Highlight Dance Show. *Albuquerque Journal*, p. A-2.

Campbell, M. (1971, March 11). Dance Group Lauded. *Rochester Democrat and Chronicle*, p. 25.

Campbell, M. (1971, March 12). Harlem Dancers Praised. *Baltimore Sun*, p. B6

Cariaga, D. (1971, February 20). Dance Theatre of Harlem in Coast Debut. *Independent Press-Telegram*, p. B2

Cohn, A. (1970), August 28). Black Ballet Troupe: Success in 3/4 Time. *Newsday (Nassau Edition)*

Glacklin, W.C. (1971, July 12). Harlem Dancers in Italy. *The Sacramento Bee*, p. A8

Harss, M. (2013). *Virginia Johnson – Artistic Director, Dance Theatre of Harlem*. Retrieved May 30, 2021, from https://dancetabs.com/2013/09/virginia-johnson-artistic-director-dance-theatre-of-harlem/

Hertelendy, P. (1972, January 14). Arthur Mitchell's Black Ballet Shows Great Promise. *Oakland Tribute*, p. 46

Howard, T. R. (2020). Dancewear Brands Get Inclusive: Six pointe shoe manufacturers commit to offering more diverse shades. *Dance Magazine*, 94(10), 16–17.

Kaufman, S. (2000, May 8). Ballet and Bootstraps. *The Washington Post*. Retrieved from http://www.washingtonpost.com

Kisselgoff, A. (1971, January 10). Harlem Dancers Excel at Guggenheim. *New York Times*, 71–.

Koch, M. (1969, March 12). The National Ballet Excels in Varied Dance Patterns. *The Sheboygan Press*, p. 13.

Latham, J. Q. (1973). *A biographical study of the lives and contributions of two selected contemporary black male dance artists-- Arthur Mitchell and Alvin Ailey--in the idioms of ballet and modern dance, respectively*. Texas Woman's University.

Lewis, E. (1971, March 9). Harlem Troupe Wins Raves on Broadway. *The Recorder*.

Links Seek Bright Youth. (1961, June). *Ebony Magazine*, p. 125.

McDonagh, D. (1969, December 6). The Dance Theater Of Harlem Offers Mitchell Excerpts. *New York Times.*

Mootz, W. (1972, February 13). Dance Theatre of Harlem Offers Electrifying Performances. *The Courier Journal & Times.*, p. A18

Muhammad, E. (1967). *How to Eat to Live.* Muhammad Mosque of Islam No. 2.

Nicsheck, M. (1971, October 11). Harlem...On Its Toes. *St. Petersburg Times*

Perpich, M. (1971, February 10). Audience Cheer Arthur Mitchell Dance Theater. *Lansing State Journal*, p. 61

Stevenson, H. (1964). *Historical Sketch of Trinidad and Tobago.* Trinidad and Tobago Gayap Organization.

Warren, J. (1970, October 18). Desires of a Black Ballerina: To Contribute, Not to Star. *The Sunday Star*, p. H

Watt, D. (1971, March 9). Harlem Dance Theatre Young, Vibrant Group. *Daily News*, p. 50.

Llanchie as a young toddler in Aruba. Photo courtesy of Aminah L. Ahmad.

With her cousin Candance (left) at four years of age. Photo courtesy of Aminah L. Ahmad.

Family gathered to see Ruby (pictured in long sleeve white jacket) and Llanchie (holding doll) leave Aruba for the United States. Photo courtesy of Aminah L. Ahmad.

Llanchie as an young teenager dancing with the Bernice Johnson Dance Studio. Photos courtesy of Aminah L. Ahmad.

Ruby, Llanchie's mother, was one of her biggest supporters. Photo courtesy of Aminah L. Ahmad.

On tour with Alvin Ailey at age seventeen. Photo courtesy of Aminah L. Ahmad

With Arthur Mitchell. Photo credit: Marbeth. Photo courtesy of the Dance Theatre of Harlem.

Dancing with National Ballet of Washington.
Photo credit: Shirley Nottingham. Photo courtesy of
Aminah L. Ahmad.

Celebrating Kwanzaa with her father Herbert in her
Washington, DC apartment. Photo courtesy of
Aminah L. Ahmad.

The late Cicely Tyson helps Llanchie with a wardrobe adjustment. Photo credit: Marbeth. Photo courtesy of the Dance Theatre of Harlem.

Llanchie's final bow as she retired from performing.
Photo credits: Marbeth. Photos courtesy of the Dance
Theatre of Harlem.

Mario and Llanchine married in 1973. Pictured with her father Herbert. Photo courtesy of Aminah L. Ahmad.

At the wedding of her daughter Mina (seated) in 2004. Pictured (L-R) Majeedah, Sara, husband Mario, Abdul-Malik, Mujahid, and Mateen.

Bethania Gomes, former Principal dancer for the Dance Theatre of Harlem at the memorial for Arthur Mitchell in 2018. Photo courtesy of Bethania Gomes.

ACKNOWLEDGMENTS

I would like to thank my mother first and foremost for allowing me to document her story in the form of this book. Thank you to Mario Ahmad for his guidance on content editing and publishing. I am grateful to Rahima Ullah for her help with proofreading and editing and to Abdul-Malik Ahmad for the cover design and image support.

While I grew up listening to my mother sharing her story, I truly enjoyed getting to know her better through talking with others. I appreciate Mrs. Marguerite Stein for allowing me to interview her about my mother's life as a child and teenager. Thank you to Tante Candy for the great insights on my family and for filling in the gaps of history. Uncle Denis always has wonderful stories to share about my grandmother and my great aunts.

I would also like to give a special note of gratitude to Anna Glass and Virginia Johnson of the Dance Theatre of Harlem for their support with photo archives. Finally, thank you to my incredible husband, Trey, for always encouraging me.

ABOUT THE AUTHOR

Mina Ahmad-Crosby is the child of immigrants from the Caribbean who converted to Islam during her infancy. Her early life was heavily influenced by her parents' dramatic shift from mainstream culture, as she was homeschooled from kindergarten until she entered college. She graduated cum laude from Georgetown University, where she spent a year studying in Cairo, Egypt. She also received Master's and Education Specialist degrees in Mental Health Counseling from the University of Florida. She is a member of Delta Sigma Theta Sorority Inc. and an active in her local Jack and Jill of America chapter. A native of Maryland, she lives outside of Phoenix, Arizona with her loving husband Trey and two children, Mezaan and Raees.

www.ingramcontent.com/pod-product-compliance
Lightning Source LLC
Chambersburg PA
CBHW062141100526
44589CB00014B/1648